BAFFLING BEHAVIOR IN THE PAST

ROAR!

LIFE IN ANCIENT EGYPT

by Noah Leatherland

T0413966

BEARPORT
PUBLISHING

Minneapolis, Minnesota

Credits
Images are courtesy of Shutterstock.com. With thanks to Getty Images, Thinkstock Photo, and iStockphoto. COVER & RECURRING – Fedor Selivanov, JORDEN MARBLE, YummyBuum, Mind Pixell. 4–5 – Sofoklo, Ewa Studio. 6–7 – hemro, Stephen Chung. 8–9 – AlexAnton, spatuletail, Daria Volyanskaya, Mikhail Gnatkovskiy. 10–11 – Andrea Izzotti, Marco Polo's Rhino. 12–13 – marseus, spatuletail. 14–15 – Samarabbas101, Miro Varcek. 16–17 – mountainpix, devil79sd, Simply Amazing, GoodStudio. 18–19 – Be Seen and Bloom, David Havel, Shanvood. 20–21 – Paolo Gallo, Egyptian Museum of Berlin, CC BY 3.0 <https://creativecommons.org/licenses/by/3.0>, via Wikimedia Commons, JoLin. 22–23 – EvrenKalinbacak. 24–25 – WH_Pics, Holger Kirk. 26–27 – Estere13, Public domain, via Wikimedia Commons, F. J. CARNEROS. 28–29 – hemro. 30–31 – Waj.

Bearport Publishing Company Product Development Team
Publisher: Jen Jenson; Director of Product Development: Spencer Brinker; Managing Editor: Allison Juda; Editor: Cole Nelson; Associate Editor: Naomi Reich; Associate Editor: Tiana Tran; Art Director: Colin O'Dea; Designer: Kim Jones; Designer: Kayla Eggert; Product Development Specialist: Owen Hamlin

Library of Congress Cataloging-in-Publication Data is available at www.loc.gov or upon request from the publisher.

ISBN: 979-8-89232-880-7 (hardcover)
ISBN: 979-8-89232-966-8 (paperback)
ISBN: 979-8-89232-910-1 (ebook)

© 2025 BookLife Publishing
This edition is published by arrangement with BookLife Publishing.

For more information, write to Bearport Publishing, 5357 Penn Avenue South, Minneapolis, MN 55419.

CONTENTS

ANCIENT EGYPT

Life in ancient Egypt was full of rich history . . . and baffling behavior! Looking back, some of the stories we hear from ancient Egypt may seem strange.

The first Egyptian **dynasty** started in 3150 BCE. However, it wasn't until 3100 BCE that the long history of ancient Egypt began.

BCE MEANS BEFORE THE COMMON ERA. THIS IS THE TIME BEFORE THE YEAR 0.

Egypt does not get a lot of rain. So, the ancient Egyptians relied on the Nile River for water. The water helped make the soil **fertile** enough to grow food.

THE NILE RIVER

Without water from the Nile River, the ancient Egyptian **civilization** would never have become as strong as it did.

GODS AND GODDESSES

Ancient Egyptians **worshipped** more than 2,000 different gods and goddesses. Each one was responsible for different parts of life and death.

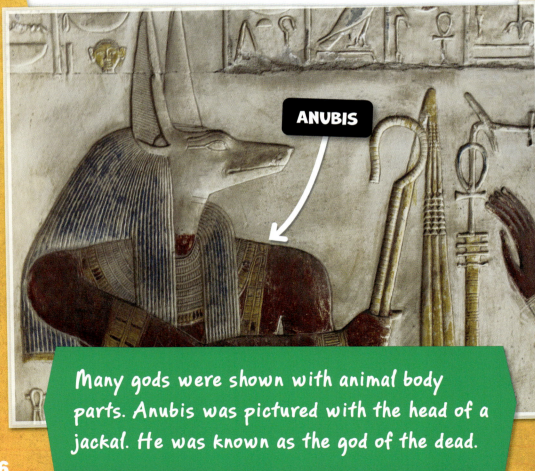

ANUBIS

Many gods were shown with animal body parts. Anubis was pictured with the head of a jackal. He was known as the god of the dead.

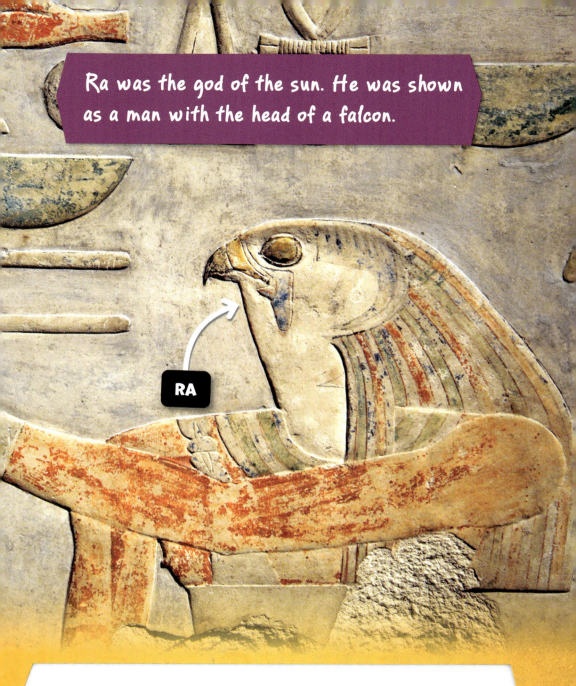

Ra was the god of the sun. He was shown as a man with the head of a falcon.

RA

The ancient Egyptians believed Ra had to fight the evil being Apep to make the sun rise. But what if the sun god lost? It would be a cloudy day!

WORSHIPPING THE GODS

The ancient Egyptians worshipped their gods in different ways. Some built temples where people could go to pay their respects. Priests looked after the temples and performed **rituals** to keep the gods happy.

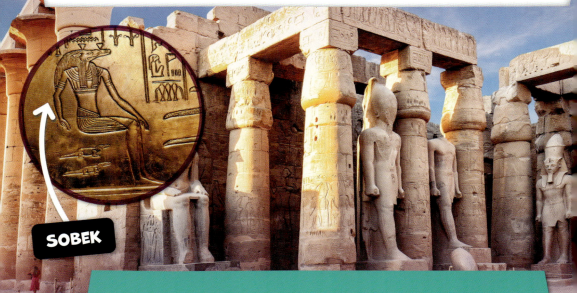

SOBEK

The god Sobek was thought to have the head of a crocodile. So, the ancient Egyptians turned dead crocodiles into mummies. Then, they placed the croc mummies in temples to please Sobek.

Instead of being **mummified**, other animals were sacrificed. The ancient Egyptians killed the animals as another way of making the gods happy.

SCARAB BEETLE IN JEWELRY

The ancient Egyptian god of the morning sun was Khepri. He is often shown as a man with a scarab head. Khepri was thought to roll the sun across the sky. But real scarab beetles actually roll balls of poop!

FEARSOME PHARAOHS

Pharaohs were the rulers of ancient Egypt. People believed the pharaohs were like gods living among humans.

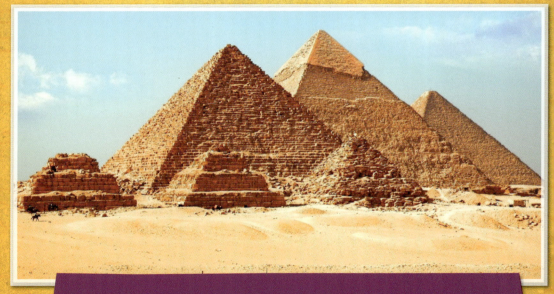

Pyramids are where some pharaohs were buried after their death. When they came to power, the first thing some pharaohs did was demand that a new pyramid be built just for them. These huge structures took many years to build.

Stories say that Pharaoh Pepi II had a not-so-sweet way of keeping flies away. He had two **enslaved** people cover themselves in honey and follow him around. The flies would buzz toward them, leaving Pepi II in peace.

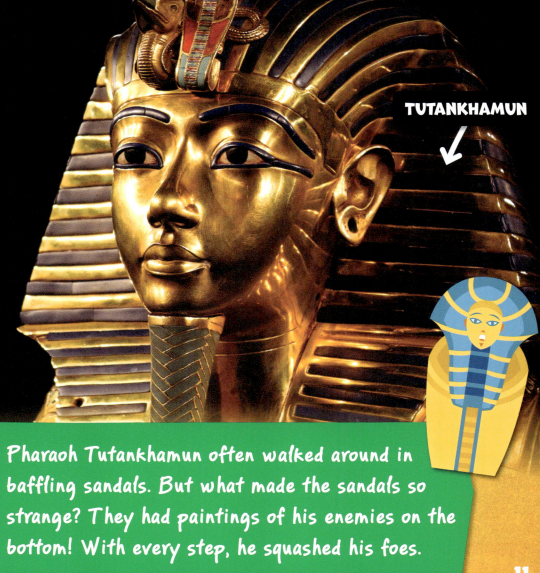

TUTANKHAMUN

Pharaoh Tutankhamun often walked around in baffling sandals. But what made the sandals so strange? They had paintings of his enemies on the bottom! With every step, he squashed his foes.

MAKING MUMMIES

Crocodiles weren't the only things mummified in ancient Egypt. When important people died, their bodies were prepared in the same way. This was thought to be a way people could reach the **afterlife**.

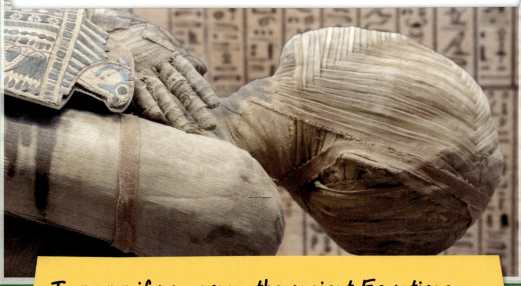

To mummify a person, the ancient Egyptians opened the body. Then, they removed the organs. The body was then filled with spices, covered in salt, and left to dry for 40 days. Finally, the ancient Egyptians wrapped the body up in cloth.

Most mummies were placed in coffins. Rich people had the money to bury their dead in sarcophagi. These expensive coffins were made of stone and shaped like people.

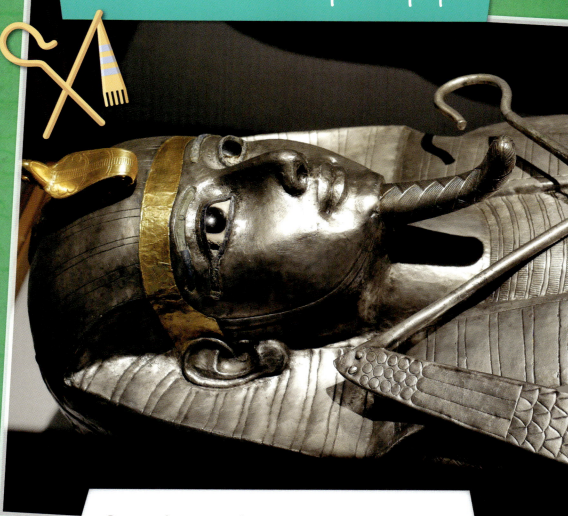

Sarcophagi could be decorated in lots of ways. Many had pictures painted on them. Some were even styled with gold.

HEALTH AND SICKNESS

Ancient Egyptians believed the human body had tubes inside. These channels were thought to help the body work properly. The Egyptians thought angry spirits could block the channels, which would make people sick.

EATING FIGS HELPED MAKE PEOPLE POOP.

To unblock the channels, ancient Egyptians believed they needed to poop! They purposely ate food that would give them diarrhea so they would poop a lot. Gross!

Ancient Egyptians often took steps to avoid getting sick. They believed magical amulets could protect them. These pieces of jewelry came in all sorts of shapes.

Doctors in ancient Egypt had a painful way of treating headaches. They would drill holes into the skull! This was thought to free any evil spirits who were causing the headaches.

PRETTY EGYPTIANS

In ancient Egypt, looking good was important. People often wore eye makeup called kohl. It not only made them look pretty, but it also protected their eyes from the sun.

Ancient Egyptians used toothpaste to clean their teeth. Unlike today, their toothpaste wasn't minty fresh. Instead, it was made from ox hooves, ashes, burnt eggshells, and stones.

Shaving your head was common back in ancient Egypt. Why? Cutting off all of your hair was much easier than dealing with head lice!

A HEAD LOUSE

What did people do after shaving their heads? They wore wigs! Wigs were often made from sheep's wool. However, rich people could also buy wigs made of human hair.

PETS OF THE PAST

Animals were also important to ancient Egyptians. Many people kept pets.

Cats were the ancient Egyptians' favorite pets. They were said to be the protectors of the house. Cats were sometimes even worshipped as gods. When pet cats died, the owners shaved their eyebrows as a sign of sadness.

According to ancient Egyptian drawings, baboons were kept as house pets, too. These large monkeys were pictured grabbing fruit. In some drawings, they played instruments!

Rich people liked to have dangerous pets. Some of them even had pet crocodiles and lions!

PLAYING GAMES

To keep themselves entertained, the ancient Egyptians created lots of toys and games. Mehen was a board game where the board looked like a curled-up snake. *Hiss!* People played with pieces shaped like animals.

SENET

Senet was a board game about reaching the afterlife. Queen Nefertiti loved the game so much that her tomb has a painting of her playing it.

One ancient Egyptian sport was similar to hockey. But instead of using a stick and puck, the ancient Egyptians used palm tree branches to strike a ball made of papyrus.

PAPYRUS PLANT

Another game that ancient Egyptians played was similar to tug-of-war. But instead of pulling a rope, they used long sticks with hooks on the end. The sticks were used to tug on a hoop.

HIEROGLYPHS

Ancient Egyptian writing was made of small pictures called hieroglyphs. A hieroglyph could **represent** a sound, a word, an object, or a feeling. Many hieroglyphs could be put together to create full thoughts or sentences.

CARTOUCHE

A	B	C	D	E	F	G
H	I	J	K	L	M	N
O	P	Q	R	S	T	U
V	W	X	Y	Z	SH	

THE NAMES OF IMPORTANT PEOPLE WERE WRITTEN INSIDE OF OVALS CALLED CARTOUCHES. WHAT WOULD YOUR CARTOUCHE LOOK LIKE?

Hieroglyphs were carved into walls and onto sarcophagi. Ancient Egyptians also used papyrus plants to make long, flat sheets similar to paper. They would write hieroglyphs on the sheets.

ANCIENT EGYPTIAN WRITING USED MORE THAN 700 DIFFERENT HIEROGLYPHS.

Not everyone could read and write in ancient Egypt. The people who could, such as priests or craftsmen, often needed the skills for their jobs.

LIFE AT HOME

Ancient Egyptians built most houses from mud. First, they shaped the mud into bricks. Then, the bricks were left to dry in the sun. Rich people lived in houses made of stone.

A WOODEN HEADREST

Most ancient Egyptians slept on the floor. Instead of pillows, they had headrests made of stone or wood.

Although ancient Egyptians worshipped some animals, they hated flies. People would put papyrus on their windows to keep out the pests. They also made a kind of flyswatter from giraffe tails.

AN ANCIENT EGYPTIAN TOILET

Ancient Egyptian houses did not have water pipes. The toilets back then were holes in the ground with stools over them.

KIDS DID WHAT?

Not all ancient Egyptian children went to school.

MOST CHILDREN DID NOT WEAR CLOTHES!

Only some boys around the age of 16 and 17 went to school. Girls, however, were not allowed to go. So, their mothers taught them skills at home.

Children who did not go to school worked with their families. Many children learned how to make clothes, grow crops on farms, or create things out of wood.

THE EYE OF HORUS WAS SAID TO PROTECT PEOPLE.

Unlike today, most people died at a young age in ancient Egypt. So, parents gave their children amulets to protect them.

BREAKING THE LAW

Ancient Egyptians took crime very seriously. Police sometimes had monkeys with them. These monkeys chased after criminals who tried to run away.

Even just seeing a crime happen could get you into trouble. Police had an unusual way of making sure **witnesses** were telling the truth about what they saw. How? They beat them up!

Ancient Egyptians believed statues of the god Amun could decide if criminals were innocent. If the statue moved one way, they were innocent. But if it moved the other way, the criminals were guilty. However, these movements were actually done by a priest hiding inside or behind the statue!

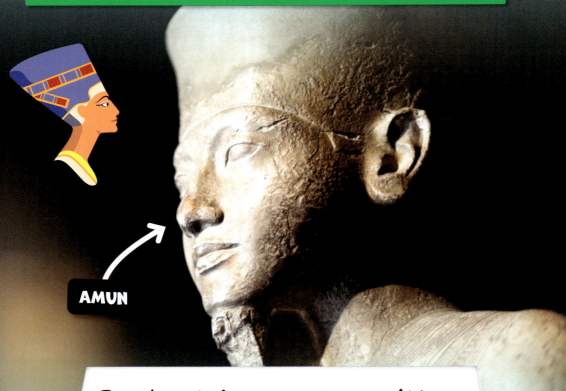

AMUN

Punishments for some crimes could be deadly. Someone caught stealing could have parts of their body chopped off. Other horrible punishments included being beaten up, stabbed, or burned alive!

YOUR PLACE IN HISTORY

Do you think you could live in ancient Egypt? From sleeping on stone pillows to brushing teeth with ox hooves and ashes, the people who lived in the past sure had it rough.

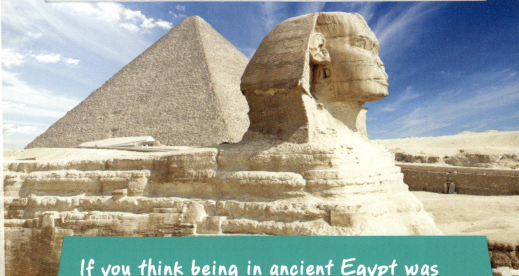

If you think being in ancient Egypt was tough, then try reading about another time period. However, be warned! Wherever you go, you may find yourself thinking . . .

what baffling behavior!

GLOSSARY

afterlife the life of a person after their death

civilization a large group of people that share the same history or way of life

dynasty a group of rulers from the same family over a long period of time

enslaved being held captive by other people and forced to work without pay

fertile able to help plants grow

mummified preserved after death to prevent a body from rotting

represent to stand for something else

rituals actions that take place during religious ceremonies

witnesses people who saw something happen

worshipped honored and respected as a god

INDEX

READ MORE

Kim, Carol. *The Secret Lives of Pharaohs (Secrets of Ancient Civilizations)*. North Mankato, MN: Capstone Press, 2025.

Mather, Charis. *The Peculiar Past in Ancient Egypt (Strange History)*. Minneapolis: Bearport Publishing Company, 2024.

LEARN MORE ONLINE

1. Go to **FactSurfer.com**
or scan the QR code below.

2. Enter "**Life in Ancient Egypt**" into the search box.

3. Click on the cover of this book
to see a list of websites.